Keeping Time

TIM DOOLEY has taught in and near London since 1974 and is Head of English and Film Studies at Rickmansworth School, Hertfordshire. He has reviewed poetry for *The Times Literary Supplement*, written obituaries for *The Times* and edited the small press magazine *Green Lines*. He has also been a creative writing tutor for the Arvon Foundation, Writers Inc and The Poetry School. His first collection *The Interrupted Dream* was published by Anvil in 1985. This was followed by *The Secret Ministry* (2001) and *Tenderness* (2004), both winners in the Poetry Business pamphlet competition. *Tenderness* was also a Poetry Book Society pamphlet choice.

Also by Tim Dooley

Tenderness (Smith/Doorstop, 2004)
The Secret Ministry (Smith/Doorstop, 2001)
The Interrupted Dream (Anvil, 1985)
Three Poems (Many Press, 1977)

Keeping Time

TIM DOOLEY

SALT

CAMBRIDGE

PUBLISHED BY SALT PUBLISHING
PO Box 937, Great Wilbraham, Cambridge CB21 5JX United Kingdom

© Tim Dooley, 2008

First published 2008

Printed and bound in the United Kingdom by Biddles Ltd, Kings Lynn, Norfolk

Typeset in Swift 9.5 / 13

ISBN 978 1 84471 333 2 hardback

Salt Publishing Ltd gratefully acknowledges
the financial assistance of Arts Council England

1 3 5 7 9 8 6 4 2

for Jo

Contents

Acknowledgements

Some of these poems have appeared previously in the following publications: *Acumen, Agenda, Ambit, Brittle Star, Chameleons, Cracked Lookingglass, Dog, Exeter Poetry Prize Anthology 1997, The Heart in Autumn, North, The North, nthposition, Numbers, The Observer, Oxford Magazine, Poetry Durham, Poetry London Newsletter, Poetry London, The Rialto, Sheffield Thursday, The SHOp, Singing Brink, Smiths Knoll, Southern Review* (USA), *Swansea Review, Tears in the Fence, Times Educational Supplement, Times Literary Supplement, Verse.*

'Brief Encounter' won fourth prize in the City of Cardiff International Poetry Competition, 1992. 'Pornography' won first prize in the 1995 Sheffield Thursday poetry competition. 'Tenderness' was a winner in the Blue Nose Poets-of-the-Year competition 2001. It is also available on the CD *Life Lines 2 : Poets for Oxfam* edited by Todd Swift.

Some of these poems appeared in the pamphlets *The Secret Ministry* (2001) and *Tenderness* (2004) as winners in the 2000 and 2003 Smith Doorstop/ Poetry Business pamphlet competitions.

My thanks are due to Tamar Yoseloff, Maurice Riordan, Maura Dooley and Andrew Waterman for instructive and supportive comments at an earlier stage in the shaping of this collection.

In the palm of my hand

Starting from the new towers' atria and in-house concessions,
    you find a way to where this yellow stone stands,
slant and widdershins, not far from the lovely naked bones of
    Catherine and William Blake. The scant
non-conformist burying ground of Bunhill Fields (hardly fields,
    neat and weeded pathways lead to the chart
that marks the graves of the remembered names)—cuts between
    trunkways hurrying noisily north of Moorgate.
Not being the man in the brown ankle-length coat who leaves a
    single flower in water here, move on to Spitalfields
past tumbled histories of housing, a church turned concert hall,
    estates and enterprises, posters stuck to walls.

Put your finger on the map and start from there, from any there,
    to see through the side window of Westminster
Public Libraries (Marylebone Branch) this intent face diving
    for the meaning his gloved finger points halfway
down the page towards. In puffa jackets, woollen hats or baseball
    caps, carrying their goods in supermarket shopping
bags, faces of all nations, hurry, saunter, cross your path, face
    or follow you. The new bagel bar. The chemists
established 1814. Blue plaques for poets in Poland Street
    and Polish *Newsweek* in the cornershops. A lowslung
bus snakes and humps round a formal square. Cream walls
    steeped in a sudden honey of late afternoon light.

And a river moves through it, walled but washing against
        the window of a Limehouse pub, alive to the warming
of the world's waters, the exchanges of currents and currency.
        Light flashes intermittently from the pyramid top
of Canary Wharf, and the yellow brown water itself is pulled
        into little peaks of reflected light. We saw it from Waterloo
Bridge on that march from Lincoln's Inn to the Imperial War Museum;
        then sat on the green lawn near those great guns
as Tony Benn shared memories of a century's dissent.
        And upriver—wisteria on white walls, gated communities,
joggers and rowers glide past a jazz club, a cricket pitch
        the entrance to a canal, public gardens, palaces.

And something like this was in his mind when he turned from
        that enormous blast, looking for those in his care
that he'd ferried through Islington and Finsbury, and saw
        twisted metal upstairs on what now looked like
a tourist bus. So that when help arrived and what could be
        made good began to be done, what was there but
to follow those walking away, westward past the dome that
        keeps Jeremy Bentham's mummified remains,
past busy hospitals beneath the telecom tower or Arab cafés
        along the Harrow Road, until somewhere near
Wormword Scrubs a stranger saw the blood on his jacket
        and helped him to the Casualty in Ducaine Road.

If we open the door, if we open our eyes, everything here
      seems paved or clothed, labelled or priced, stamped
with its destination, encrypted with its time of arrival.
      It is the sidelong looks more in recognition than
desire that release the unchanelled: the palest hint of
      a blush, sky in the mirrorglass of offices, what
a girl called 'that Thomas Hardy kind of foolishness'.
      The bite of the pickled chilli in the pitta salad
in Gig's fish bar in Tottenham Street has it. The heron
      standing on the effluent pipe looks out for it.
Daily we brush against it or glimpse it beyond our touch.
      What we walk through, fail to say, or try to hold.

The length of spring

Peace is possible. The Amnesty dove's
still stickered to the window of the house
we didn't buy from you. And now you're housed
in a wicker coffin, a hamper of
the good things you were and will be, in the love
of your still friends, in the Friends' meetinghouse.
We stay to watch your children shoulder the spades
they dug into the moist earth to cover you;
and talk as if words could recover you
to the cold air, to the light's sharpest blades.

The same fierce brightness picks out the parade
against the war, and we remember you
at the month's end as we move shoe and shoe
ahead along the Embankment, early
arrivals buying new badges, nearly
losing one another by Westminster tube
and dawdling down Whitehall, enjoying the true
absurdity of *Make Tea Not War*. Dearly
the young in black entwine themselves for warm,
lest love fail, should nothing stop the war.

Another world is possible. As the war
draws near, a slogan on a lapel draws
smiles and nods, but subdued by will and force
we stumble in. I block out the war,
listening to Jacobi's *Iliad* not the news,
until the statues start to fall across
the screens and grudging praise of 'moderate loss'
is heard beyond the dusty haze
of crazed cuneiform tablets, wrecked houses
and orphaned children's distanced cries.

Cellular

We'd grit our teeth in trains as the brash
human resources manager turned the seat
next to us into her office, or blush
as privacies invaded
our poorly air-conditioned space.

But we had also seen a strong jaw soften,
a head tilting towards its own shoulder,
murmuring to the small world
it cradles and creates. And smiled
as the straight-faced colleague
danced in the car park,
her head back, laughing
like someone living on another plane.

And later would hear how,
in Manhattan, a husband tapped again
the digits he had tried to reach all day
beneath rubble, atoms, ashes, dust
until the voice mail's memory could take
no more spoken words or text.

Digital

Like a girl with a new pony,
she's happy enough to pose
for the lens. The fun's on pause

but it's something for the folks
at home; a souvenir of the tour
to speed ahead of her on-line.

It's asked of her; she looks
almost bored in her boyish
t-shirt and camouflage pants,

which is so like a uniform,
it takes a while to see
the casual clothes are army

issue. This is a dog-lead
not a bridle. This is no
pony, just a naked man.

The TPA Bar

The door frames its establishing shot, lit
by the last June afternoon: the glitter of
rained-on pavement punctuated by platform
heels, instrument cases and, as backdrop,
the guitar shop with the sign for drum lessons
upstairs. The girl from Australia in period
makeup tells the room: *I'm in a race
with my wallet.* They're smoking their

last cigarettes. We're feeding the jukebox,
in this little bubble from the last century,
looking only now and then at the soundless
screen with its strapline *Breaking News*
and a car in flames entering the terminal,
guessing the songs from their first few chords.

In the Street

Sometimes he's tired of being a man.
The reflection he sees, in shopwindows
or the cinema screen, takes on a sad
substance, tired and withered: ash-stains
on a shiny piece of suit cloth.

The gents hairdressers, with its cocktail
of smells, stings him to tears.
He wants the sleep of wool or old stones,
to see nothing of enterprises or gardens,
nothing of merchandise, spectacles, lifts.

He's tired of his feet, of toe-clippings,
of hair everywhere. Of his shadow.
He's just tired of being a man,
waking like a root in a dark cellar,
absorbing, thinking, counting the dead.

And Monday is the screech of a tyre,
or a sudden petrol flare.
It sees him coming with his prison face,
sends him to hospitals where bones fall out of
the windows, to damp and vinegary stores.

So he walks around, for peace, for forgetfulness,
past caged birds the colour of sulphur, tripe,
dentures in a coffee pot, surgical appliances,
and old men's underclothes hanging from a line,
weeping their slow, dirty tears.

Y Habra Trabàjo Para Todos

Canary, scarlet, oatmeal, azure, green.
I like the green best I think—the colour
of a young leaf or just ripe capsicum—
used here for half a face, or the profile
of a face, all but the pouch under one eye
that masquerades as a full-bellied dove.

A woman's bare arm—impossibly long—
unfolding sheaves of wheat, posters, what might be
rolls of cloth; more faces split by stalks; a clenched
fist clutching a flashlight or pick-handle,
holding up, in the patchy blue,
the bright lonely star of his country's flag.

Among the waxy cookery smears and jagged
blu-tack scars on our uneven kitchen wall,
the caption's bold lettering survives
with this ambiguous promise; for sixteen years
it's earned its place—this message from Allende's
republic—AND THERE WILL BE WORK FOR ALL.

The briefcase

in brown leather
your father gave
me after that last
but one illness
has worn grey
near the handle;
only one strap
fastens now, the
other dangling
useless. It is an
occasion to take
it out, as if a relic,
to feed and polish
it with creams,
placing these few
loose sheets of
paper on either side
of the divide.

Itinerants

In this wrecked country
where dry stone walls
once half built, now
half fallen, protect
nothing badly—you
wonder how it is
the people live. Wind
tears at leaf-stripped
trees and rain bares
rock of a soil that's
scarcely natural.

The van rattles,
rasping with Irish
on this fourth day
of storm. Packs on
separate shoulders,
we neither touch
nor quarrel. I watch
your tongue tracing
the margin of your
mouth as if a smile,
or something, were
suddenly to begin.

The Milky Way

The marble features of the Parthenon frieze
        aren't the only things
to seem flatter and greyer since the summer
        you were sixteen.

O'Driscoll remembers the white bicycles
        those other Provos
left on Amsterdam street corners for free
        and common use.

There were pictures from museums on the train
        and songs of that time
in the background, the five days we crossed
        from the Stedelijk

to Jordaan's brown cafés. It was later though,
        with wanted posters
for the Red Army Fraction pasted on a wall
        at the terminus.

There were screams in the night, soft cheese
        and jam at breakfast.
A tape of Bukka White barely troubled the
        glittering meniscus

of your genever, or the couple chopping a black
        cube into silver-
paper deals: their downy daughter snoozing
        on the bar.

We shared a four bunk room with transients
        waiting to buy a car.
Stavros and his cousin were ready to go home
        —after a decade

in New York, struggling with electronics and
                English, repairing
beat-up radios, lecturing on Ritsos—to go home
                to the free use

of their tongue. O'Driscoll is easing his way
                into the story
of his second time in Holland—peace week
                at the Melkweg.

Did his disarmament play leave the audience stunned
                or were they stoned,
like the actors, staring at significant intervals
                between words?

He wants to tell us about the boat-trip back to Hull,
                how they disposed
of the stuff—fear and the North Sea at night.
                I am looking

in your eyes at a different year and the dark
                sea off Naxos,
a high glittering sky and its reflection,
                like a window

opening in our marriage, the evening's gifts
                scattered freely,
like the broad and unmourned highway
                of spilt milk.

June

The first weeks of Wimbledon
     and the word 'love'
has passed between us like
     zero, or some chosen
absolute. That ochre picture
     —sunpainted Italy—
a trail snapped from a mountain
     in your teens, now
stained by late development
     is in my eye again.

Those first times away from him
     look empty and unfinished,
as we sort your father's things
     and the word 'alone'
opens like a blister in the earth.

Preparing to meet the day

A routine and a rite—
this soaping, scraping away
of the night's crop of maleness.

Rinsing the blade,
as if concealing the evidence—

he catches, in the air,
rank nicotine and silence.

His hand on her shoulder
is no help at all.

A relic from that time
they looked together at the light
we move through, and towards.

September

He's begun reading biographies
and noticing how the cramped
early pages, the three
contrasting accounts
of how the lovers met

give way to vaguenesses,
gaps filled with speculation,
years when the subject might
have visited Tuscany
or acted in an undistinguished role

of which records later vanished.
So, after Sunday lunch,
it seems natural to walk
through the park unnoticed,
or watch others wander past

without acknowledgement,
kicking a crab apple perhaps,
or prising a conker open,
exposing its shiny
coffin-shaded fruit.

Resistance

Days after the storm, this unsought fog
holds fireworks' aftersmoke, while streetlights blink
a wasteful orange forgetful of clocks.

Yellow and pale and brown, our hectic walk
to school fills with fragmented leaves,
faces passing, familiar multitudes.

And Shelley was wrong too about the way
the dying leaves hold to the damaged branch
against the force of theory or wind.

Leaves cling like all of us, to purposes
imagined once—the wound forgotten spring
still uncoiling in our steps.

Mrs. Wu

In '57, he went to see the new Russian.
The great helmsman said, *Rap the guy's knuckles.*
That's no way to behave when Joe ain't hardly dead.
Destalinize . . . Destabilize!
And Enlai said to Kruschev,
You've taken too much land.

The fat peasant called him bourgeois.
Zhou was still smiling.
Who says we've nothing in common?
We've each betrayed our class.
And he told the story and heard it told again
in Warsaw, Budapest, Belgrade . . .

Two years before in Bandung:
We must not forget, as Asians,
the first atom bomb fell on our continent . . .

You know those stories. Long before,
my husband called him blood brother
and paid for his study in Kyoto.

He knew too little Japanese
and, with nothing to spend, took
the woman's part,
clearing the futon and sweeping the room.

In the evenings, we ate what he cooked.
He clung to the wine bottle and argued with Wu.
A strong leader is worthless, unless the people learn.
'And what is strong drink worth?', I asked.
Zhou looked for a broom and next day brought me flowers.

There was blossom for nine days in Maruyama park.
Now nowhere in Kyoto is that bittersweet scent.
Many died. Too many with his name on.
And he too died early, before Zedong,
the word *poems* ambiguous on his lips.

The Cavalcantine Lure

A pretty face, the very heart of reason,
the expert's dry indifference to rank,
the song of birds and lovers' reasoning
and boats lit all along the southern bank.
Purest air; dawn's first whitest hour
and white snow falling where there is no wind,
backwaters and meadows gemmed with flowers
—gold and silver with sea-blue gems inlaid.

Match such, the poet says with your spare praise
of love, or the one who's loved, and his words
are red-hot coals that we can walk across;
like sunlit metal, the pealing bells heard
clearly in the twilight of years and days
with talk of songs and stings, of heart and loss.

Song

I passed the warning signs.
My skin was scratched with briars.
I found the hidden lake
where the heron's wing caught fire.

My skin was scratched with briars.
My cuffs were grey and torn.
Where the heron's wing caught fire
I felt as if transformed.

The surface glittered red and green
beyond the boundary wire
as if a sparkling stone
nestled in my palm.

Beyond the boundary wire,
I found the hidden lake
nestling, in my palm,
beyond the warning signs.

Southerly

Sweet knowingness, a crystal fog goodbye,
swordstrokes almost in silence, bladelight veiled.
He praises the grey tone in the voice that
wavers in the distant reaches of song.
Lost song. And beyond its pure form trembles
a further song. Light and the death of light—
and a note higher than passion or pain.
A real place in the unreal stream.

Her voice moves in its own space, and moves too
in his mind that drifts between banks, knowing
extremes. Somehow I've turned up next to him,
outside the closed museum, imagining
the apple tree burning with magic, the
miniature marbles cold in the vitrine.

Tityus

In Michelangelo's drawing
this voluptuous male reclines,
one hand tied to a pillow of stone
while the other seems to slide below
the belly of the broad-spanned,
muscular, soft-feathered bird.
Daily it pecks his liver,
sensuality's last square.
Nightly his strength returns.

Stanley walks around the frame
to see the figure traced again.
On the verso it emerges
a resurrected Christ.

On a preserved railway platform,
a dozen years ago,
he saw a kiss between women:
a face upturned, something
half suppressed, half understood,
hanging like steam in air,
compressed like veins in rock.

For Ernest Seigler

I came across your books last week
in the Ealing Oxfam,
Rilke's *Orpheus* in the New York
first edition of the German text

that will keep as a gift
for Christmas. A Robert Frost
I knew, but didn't know:
A Witness Tree. (I couldn't give

somehow, good money for
the Ronald Bottrall from
Tambimutti's press. But
took the Sidney Keyes.)

There they were, with your name in ink
and '46 in subscript.
So in the dying days of this year,
sixty years after

you spent hard earned,
I'd guess, cash
at Better Books, 92–
94 Charing + Road,

I noticed the tiny
bookplate for the shop
and, turning a page,
the line drawing of Frost,

youngish for his fifties
and already outliving
the poet friend his
face here reminds me of.

The poem I read on to
speaks of a 'day
no shadow
crossed but ours'.

And today is set fair
to unravel as such
another movement
from clear clearly to clear:

the sun mirrored
by the river's small waves,
music like a muffled joy
playing in a back room.

Such easy heigts or depths
give form to what is passing
some sense of compensation
for 'what it lacks in length'.

Delivery

(i.m. Michael Donaghy)

Five minutes into your memorial
service, my knee is jiggling to
a reel you wrote at twenty-five,

half your life away. My memory
and ear struggle to end the line
Donne wrote for such as you. You'd

find the word, as easy as breathing out:
rest of their bones and soul's (   )
four syllables; something to rhyme with free.

Seeing Shelley Plain

The tall figure with feathering
white hair, crossing the foyer
of the Queen Elizabeth Hall
as if on castors, one arm aloft
holding the largest glass of vodka
in the world, as if this were
the Statue of Liberty's lamp
(and he Paul Revere)
was Robert Lowell.

And when the Poetry Society flunky
added to his censure of flashes
that smoking was not permitted,
Auden's dried apricot face snarled
that he liked cigarettes,
but cameras interfered with his reading.
And what a reading. Parts of the Eddas.
'In Praise of Limestone'. Favourites back to the thirties.

You could get Bunting then.
Briggflatts almost too often,
but *Chomei at Toyama* unforgettably
and 'a piece W. B. Yeats did me the honour
of learning by heart'.
Somehow, in the downstairs bar,
we got to talking about how Homer
would have fared on the wireless.

I never saw Stevie Smith (though
my brother did) and I later met people
who'd met David Jones. At college
I vaguely knew a man called Trueblood
who in Venice, on his way from Santa Barbara,
saw almost the last of Ezra Pound,
silent between two aged women.

The Folding Star

Let's not ask if this is the last time
we watch the sea off the Eastern coast
erode the land, wave by grasping wave.
Look instead through the pimpled panes
at the firm red glow of evening light
on brick. Lift your eyes and wait until
the deepening blue reveals a pinch
of light, a planet-shaped white promise.

While we talk, hours gather to take flight.
In a neglected space where children
wander, we've seen wild Eden-coloured
fruit projected on a wall, fruit a
poet grew from seed resisting the
damage of geography and time.

The Next Poem

The new shelves are in place; so what goes back on
them has become the debate. Do *Jack Straw's*
     Castle and *The Doors of Stone* stay
       on the living writers' shelf, or move

somewhere higher? All of which is a displacement of,
or preamble to, the more unsettling question:
     what will fit in the slim gaps they leave?
      You told me how your friend drew you

a diagram of our latest and brightest best, using
different coloured pens to show the links—who
     published, prized, or who shagged who.
      A pretty spirograph flower; at its heart

another emptiness. Are we waiting for something
more feral to cartwheel its way out of Zennor,
     with a faint whiff of whalemeat and whiskey?
      Or a cool intelligence from east of Cape Cod

to murmur our nerves to order? Not knowing where
the next poem is coming from may be a virtue of
     sorts; we can sit out here on the pier,
      wearing caps that sailors use to shade

their eyes against the evening glare and look for
shapes emerging from the deep, or listen out as
     some lost air from the hinterland, faltering but true,
      prepares its passage through the lips.

Snow Days

In a week where you wake at half three
three days in a row, and even the water
which ought to spiral down gaily
beneath your feet in the shower, won't
but rises greyly to your shins before
slipping shamefacedly away, it's alright
to hope for the morning call that says:
Forget about today. We don't need you

to come in. And the children head for the hill
with trays as toboggans. And the young have
coloured scarves and hats to stand out against
the white surprise of everything, while we
slide back beneath covers enjoying what is
known and warm and feels like righteous sin.

Détente

A fingertip at play
inside you and my head
cushioned on your breast,
listening like a safe breaker
for some loosening
of the latch.

The thin ice has melted
and the gate's unlocked on
the bridge to the lake's small island,
where rock plants flower—saxifrage
or snowdrops waving tiny
flags of truce.

The Unburdening Room

A wooden
structure about
the size of a
gardening shed
in which a
window is fixed
open for native
wildflowers, a
yawning chasm,
but as well
the voices you
crossed a city not
expecting to hear.
Beside the stream
leaves leak like
eggs through
brown paper.
The rocks the
river runs
through are walls
of a disused mill.

She heard
something in the
music driving
back to England
a week ago like
voices out of
childhood. The
Sunday Latin he
reeled away
from, grey stone
against an
unrelieved grey
sky. When rain
relents, light
touches a patch
of skin or grasses
shift with the
prevailing wind,
an accidental
nimbus rewards
the patient stare.

Conduit

A stone's throw
from Fleet
Ditch the
plastic cup of
wine taken
from me and a
face I start to
recompose
*We are Nabis
of the text.* Mr
4 a.m.'s dark
glasses share a
flat December
surface with
poems of failed
marriage, a
balcony open to
night's cries,
flecks in the
retina, urine
examined for
portents.
*It has been
taken from me,*
the beautiful
skin tones of
the young, gull-
shrieks off the
Atlantic,
a child lost in
walkways of
dapple grey.

Sleepwalker's Romance

Shoes were at the heart of it. That much was clear.
Luxurious shoes of all-assuaging suppleness.
And he had left them there. Wherever there was.
With the picnic stuff in the precinct or the shopping bags
on the hilltop. And now he was here. And here
was also subject to change at a moment's notice.
The back of a Morris Minor or the restaurant at Fortnum's.
But wherever here was, they were. Welcome and comforting.
His children. His parents. This or that beloved?
But the only shoes on offer were a pair of beat-up trainers.
Not Reeboks exactly. Never mind the fur-lined slipper.
So he had to head off along the hostile corridors.
The playground was wet and it was becoming dark
earlier than expected. And there were questions to answer.
He realised that by now someone else could have the shoes.
And he might never know if it was power or it was love.
That he was running from. That he was searching out.

Class

Alvin's red Pringle
is well the business
and Shital's Kappa top
rumoured to be crucial.

Carrie was telling Keri
all about Mu Lin's double
reverse tuck into seatdrop
when the bell went.

I blew the whistle. Now
I watch the last, the least
keen forms shuffle
into the building,

before the gulls'
shrieking sharp descent,
white-grey against grey-black
from corners of the roof,

investigating crisp packets—
one frantic group tearing
apart an unfinished roll.
Soon I'll be hurrying back

where this shared serious
business goes happily,
noisily on: maiming,
remodelling our words

Afterwards

The ritual of open-evening wall-displays.
In the maths corridor, she came on neatly-shaded graphs,
histograms, colour-coded pies. *Our Leisure Time.*
TV, homework, shopping, sports and games
jostling with visits to friends and paper rounds.

On Raymond's bar chart, a single column towered above
its neighbours' dwarfish blocks, its simple label *Out.*
It didn't take her long to bring to life from that
an image of the gangly, crop-haired boy, dangling
on a swing too small for him, in the wet and leafstrewn park.

And it seems no time has passed when, in an unfamiliar pub,
a voice calls out, *Remember me, Miss!*
He tells her how he went back to show them all:
his uniform, the noise his boots made on the tiling floors.
Mr. Jones said, let us know before, another time.

He expected Ireland, got the Gulf. *There's lots of stuff
you never hear about. This big ditch we dug* . . . Afterwards
he got out quick. Health reasons. But the training gets you work.
Security. Firearms' research. *But I was always clumsy, miss.*
He gestures with his splintered lower arm.

A Postcard from the Fifties

In summer of course, hearing the estuary birds screech and announce
an arrival of light on the khaki mudflats. The eye-stinging glimmer
of birth. And the town streets still gap-toothed from bombs. To arrive
in New York then would be to wear another hat: the bebop backdrop,
paint dripped on canvas. Or coming off the boat here, to Southampton—
after the shipboard romance—as if your exile was over, and
language let you back to its source. And only later the closed doors,
the cards in windows regretting your landing.

Camus, Golding, Oe agree: something is rotten in the heart's
systole and diastole—the expansive desire and the shrinking
back. Shadows fixed to a pavement, pleasure off in some
institutional siding, skewered with a butcher's tag to the
Gingham cloth. The heroics last for a while—dignity reserved
for topping-out rituals in new towns, founding of scholarships.
You downed state orange juice and cod-liver oil, expected of—
never to know their listing, and counting of, loved names.

How early the curly-headed, smiling child pushing the dog on
wheels, learned the prosody of defeat: eyes turned away, laughter
cut with a phrase. There is a whole language to be learned:
what can be touched and seen; what can be imagined with a map;
what is invisible or forbidden to touch. To move out of this with
a handstand or tackle to the legs, a splatter of colour or stars
and glue, a list of the capitals of Europe, the tidal wave of the
cinema screen, a prayer learned by heart—was accepting a gift.

Chez Haynes

Leroy Haynes, an Alabaman on a G.I. tour,
enjoyed these open streets where you could
face a white man eye to eye and not say 'sir'
or tip your head. Football player, actor,
sociologue and cook—Haynes turned a new
tongue to the lilt of the South and organised.

He set up his soulfood kitchen in Montmartre.
The photos on the wall of the jazz greats
and fifties movie stars trumpet his success;
Baldwin, Chester Himes and Richard Wright
argued the protest novel in Haynes Grill.
Tonight the singer and guitarist play 'Yesterdays'

In back, his Portuguese widow, Maria,
prepares pan-fried sausages, or ham hocks
and gabbage with cornbread on the side.
She lets the D.C. girl wait tables, looking in
shyly now and then to see what small
differences a life makes in the crowded world

Tenderness

Is it six weeks since he started to scan
the green perimeters of towns like these,
skirt small-scale neighbourhoods for playing fields
whose mists give way to the thin metal legs
of institutional tables? Today he walks
along a gaping line of opened hatches—
Volvo Estates or sun-roofed Sierras—
noting cardboard-housed crockery, batches
of film magazines, one ironing board
burn-stained, little-worn suits and dresses.
He's looking, if asked, for electrical goods
but has in mind a certain twin-tone box,
coated in thin plastic, latched like luggage,
he'll recognise even from this distance.

The cream loudspeaker grille might be badly
yellowed, or chipped near one of its curved
corners, but he'll pull out a sheaf of notes.
He'll take the Dansette home and then search out
(among loft debris, dusty mementoes
of his children's childhood) the paper bags
that store—some scratched and most in mismatched
sleeves—his old black vinyl discs.

                    Sifting
Parlophone pound signs, ears labelled
eff eff double r, he'll select eight singles
to stack on the still shiny central spindle
and shift the arm across.

                Then he'll notice
he's chosen Soul records mostly: dance
numbers where the word *man* repeats itself
or gets stretched across three bars by Percy Sledge.
None of them stick or jump and the last brings
Otis Redding's voice, soaring pure against
the tinny unimpressive backing sound,
imploring him to *try a little*. And that word.

Echoes

They called it the second summer of love
but they dressed as if for the first.
Clive's sawdust-red hair hung lank
and long as Zal Yanovsky's and
Indira peered at the Browning essay
that poked out of her copy of Vogue
through Janis Joplin's specs.

Even their teacher, pushing forty,
could risk a narrow paisley-patterned tie.
A late September sun blessed
the afternoon and their lesson took that light.
Passion outraced wit as the first act closed;
the hall and imagined hills rang
to Olivia's, Viola's reverberate love.

One had the wild hair and quizzing eyes of
Tim Buckley on the cover of *happy sad*.
He had too much to say at first,
started coming late, missed lessons,
disappeared for weeks, returned
and half explained. Promises were made.
He vanished once again.

He sent a postcard from New York:
dog-sitting in a loft. Then home
and hospital. Was it the drugs they said
he sold that fired his brain?
The gossiping air knew best. He came
for a reference with his Macedonian girlfriend;
each of them a gentle refugee.

Yes it is

It was something to do with the two of us
learning to drive so late; and that collection
of misplaced singles, B-sides, E.P. tracks

and oddities like *Komm, Gib Mir Deine Hand*
came with us on our first car trip across country.
The A40. Dennis Potter's road. From Metroland

past Oxford, stopping at Birdlip to glimpse blue
remembered hills, picnicking in the Forest of Dean,
then down through valley-heads to my parents' home.

There were moments of terror: an articulated
lorry pulling into our lane just as we passed
its tail-gate; and anxieties about direction,

and moments of dreadful fatigue. The boys
counted legs of pub signs. And the tape helped :
the early songs most. Ringo's *Matchbox*

holding his nose, *jealous* rhyming with *as well as*
over a repeated rhythmic chord, and then
that song nobody quite recalled, as if it had been

lying in wait for our early middle age.
Three-part harmony. John and George
obliterating Paul, Liverpool masking Detroit.

Red and *blue* and the unspoken *black*,
as Lennon's voice splintered in the bridge,
mourning his mother as you mourned yours.

Brief Encounter

Bonking in Rome,
Goethe tapped hexameters on his mistress's back.
O'Driscoll thought of home,
listening out for the tickety-clack
of rail and wheel that wasn't to be heard
in the air-conditioned carriage.

His fingers worked a brief massage
through the shaggy beard that just
resisted grey. Then a quick
double slap to the cheeks, to wake
himself—or get the touch at least
of something real.

He turned his gaze away from the rail
to the imaginary face
of Eva, his companion. She traced
a letter in the moistened vapour
you don't get in trains these days. *J'ai peur*,
she would have said, had she been French.

But she was American. And language
loped away from her in long arching swirls,
even and intelligent,
naming what went past, examining what was meant
by the latest curl and turn
in what was surely not the march of events.

O'Driscoll considered a sandwich,
observed a chalk horse stretched out against
ancient greenery, and thought
of generations who crept down from hill-forts
to scrape the grass away—their unfenced
world—and what he still called the mind of Man.

The flare of Eva's lucent mind
guttered momently; and he was rising, breathless,
to the story of that Dorset giant, taller
than some cathedrals, with its enormous . . . *No, a phallus,*
she intercepted briefly
a penis is a great deal smaller.

And he had made her up to cut him down.
Fantastic irony. The train stayed on the track.
all he could do was read his paperback,
sharing romantic sorrows with Young Werther.

Another Part of the City

It was dark. He was wet and half a mile west
of where he was meant to be. So he dried out,
nursing a pint of mottled, off-brown best
in the back lounge of a bar that had been named
for some Crimean battle. The street had been lined
with recent cars and fairly healthy trees.

Inside was the usual plush, brasses and polished
wood—and the usual talk he supposed: office
politics, purchases, a hint about creosote, the match;
and an odd running joke about a man called Pritchard.
Pritchard was nothing to him. He would never get the hang
of his story, never know why Godalming was funny or important.

He had tried Pork Scratchings, tried an interest in cricket.
Now he sat with his back to the wall and a pencil
for the crossword. It was beginning to trickle through—
what Eva had told him at the party in Dulwich.
What it means for your face not to fit. To be moon-featured
or differently complexioned, with the magazines gorgeously gaunt.

Or what Gregor had said about his first trip back
in the early days of the thaw. Exhausting welcomes
and a bloke who could tell from his face the exact suburb
his father and uncle had fled from. Not particularly clever.
You needn't know anything about visas or fear—just where the Jews
were likely to have lived. He was getting the message.

It was dark. He was dry, but half a mile west
of where he was meant to be. So he drained down
the remains of his mottled, off-brown best
and left his paper, clueless, on the sagging chair.
It was just that he was off course. Not the weather,
not the map. Pritchard, Godalming. And unfamiliar trees.

Edit

You could start rumours about rivals and substantiate them.
Invert the corporate planner's wall-chart. Secrete his fresh
pack of Post-Its in the marketing manager's drawer.
Then wait for the many-headed snake to do its surreptitious worst,
insinuating between desk and VDU, sliding behind vertical files,
past the *monstera* no one bothered to water.
Prepare to profit, to be amused, to forget the whole thing.

At the end of lunch, instead of getting up from the table, and sneaking
half-reluctantly like the others back to your parking place,
linger with that magnificent she or he who switched the earth's
magnetic poles back then. Stay all afternoon, with a print
of the harbour at Mykonos, some fruit and drying bread.
Stay after the serious drinking, the singing, the talk of running away.
Stay as the foolish drinking starts.

But it would be wrong!
Some repeated phrase or loop you didn't recognise straight off.
As you sand your palms with stubble, facing the washroom mirror,
it becomes monstrously clear that this is Nixon's voice.
The background's different silence
tells you the phrase was recorded later,
spliced into the tape to disguise guilt.

Narcissus

Neither sliding request-slips
across the central desk,
nor making tall, curved shelves
his point of landfall
as he pilots himself back
to a numbered, lettered space
beyond the stretching spokes
of others' loaded tables

—returning to his text
is when the word *reflection*
suggests itself; and tapping
some quiet rhythm on his teeth
with a pencil, it becomes
imposed on his regard.

The face that swims towards him—
breaking a surface of language
a hundred and forty years
seem scarcely to have troubled—
is no other than his own.
where else to find repeated
the shameful hesitations,
the penetrating stare?

Was the great half-globed room
—silent mill of learning—
all set up for this?
Dusty hand-held mirrors
peered at for a second glimpse
of our own returned desire?

A bell rings. Readers shuffle into line.
A man in jeans and gold-rimmed specs
hands back a lightly annotated Plath.
The elegant, tall woman ahead
keeps her Napoleon on hold.

Books crash on trolleys,
disappear to stacks.
The legendary echo
is what disturbs him most.

Directive

There will be no dogs.
Muscle relaxant techniques developed in the clean cities campaign
to go national. Private sponsorship will match
innovation capital in sheep-herding areas.

The public role of Corgis to be phased out.
Also increased competition for heritage manufacturers.
Alternatives to Elgar to be encouraged.
The new anthem: *A Nation now and then.*

The new religion: spiritualism.
Replace that back-street, ouija-tapping fraud
with a customer-focused chain. Agree quality thresholds
for contact with the dead, service length and ectoplasm.

And horticulture rationalised.
The unlovely rose uprooted, its antisocial thorns burnt on hilltop beacons,
seeds pulverised, different-shaded petals shredded,
making the land free for order and light.

Pornography

The day was ending. Darkening air
    would soon take home from labour each
    animal that walks the earth. On this field too
feet stamped. Misty skeins of breath
    rose from glistening lips like Mackay's
    whose tongue lolled now over his lower teeth
as he eyed the ball for the place-kick.
    His team mates were taller and more fair
    than Donnelan's broad-shouldered, brown-stubbled
brutes. Consider, for example, their
    saggy-buttocked lock as the scrum breaks.
    Consider the flapping breeze-blown folds of fat
on pumping stumpy legs as he retreats.
    Consider this; and then compare the pale
    blue-veined marble of our three-quarter's firm
muscled upper thigh, glimpsed when he
    feeds the ball back from a further maul.
    Note the stud-marks bloody there, for neither team
is entirely naked. Note the hooker's
    commitment to the game, how, breaking away,
    he cuts down space, runs, swerves and keeps possession.
Note his mastery of grubber, chip and punt.
    Rewind the tape. For this is more than just
    another of O'Driscoll's stories. Try to ignore
the penny-sized needle bruises in close-up.
    None of our men are users. Scorn our opponents'
    chilled pillocks. Celebrate flesh returned to its element
of earth, the insistent inscription of rain.

Out

Lucille had the letter in her bag and *gratitude, rightsize,*
leaner strategy, corkscrewed in her mind,
as she took the stairs in twos, took the leave owing her,
left quickly, taking the stairs again, in no particular order.
She took the tube to where she'd left the car,
slunk in and, glancing up and left,
moved into traffic. She ventured vaguely northward.
Kilburn State, the Welsh Harp reservoir, slipped past to one side.
When Jazz FM faded, she scrambled, one hand in the shoe box,
for a tape. Not Gorecki. Not Neil Young Unplugged.
She fished for the cassette Khaleb had taped in Cairo.
Umm Khaltoun's plaintive singing. Rhythm and voice
passionate, unyielding, unintelligible to her
as she blocked out Hertfordshire. She found herself
in Hitchin, paid and displayed, considered her position, found
nothing useful to her but a poached egg and tea.
And yet continued, eastwards now, garden-ribbon pseudo-cities
opening to tall skies of the broad East Anglian plain
somewhere near Wallington, where Eric Blair was wed
and saw, near Manor Farm, a cart horse bullied by a boy.
She skirted Cambridge heading North, suppressing a regret,
attaining speed on dual-carriage A-roads,
dodging horse-boxes, seeing airfields to her right, slowing
to fields in harvest and Swaffham's Georgian square,
still unsatisfied, still not knowing what she sought.

Near Walsingham an older world erupted:
Gothic arches bare as neolithic bones, prayer-filled,
sanctimonious sanctuaries. She shivered, heading for the coast.
Between Wells-next-the-Sea and Sheringham, she bought
a ticket for the motor boat that takes you out

into the brown waters south of Blakeney Point,
where oyster catchers dive for food
and the diamond-glittering, brown-and-grey-skinned seals,
swivel and swim between sand bank and Arctic sound,
nurturing their young, adapting like the coastline to the tide.

A Salesman in the Lakes

West. Waste. Wastwater with its shifting scree
stirs in Stanley's inner eye, as he stops for petrol
south of Cleator Moor, noting the No to Nirex signs,
but thinking of the play: *Inside His Head.*

The abandoned title sends him back to the primal scene,
the bare boards in the blue box by Derwentwater,
the simple table where son and father fight.
Stanley remembers where he first heard these words.

Too big to fit on the 405 lines of the family screen,
the monstrous father raged. Stanley applauded
the younger Loman's cry. *You fake. You phoney little fake.*
Now Stanley knows too well the heaviness

that lumbers from small deception to unmeant mistake.
Arriving at last, he checks publicity, bookings,
trying to forget the image of a man who looks like him,
slumped in a lay-by, asleep, he hopes, at the wheel.

The Hammer

He wandered gobstruck
through the Dublin day
at just the thought of it.
Some sky of beaten brass
shining like the surface
of an ornamental gong.
That tall woman's looks,
an escaping phrase,
the bordered continent,
all beaten, beaten down
like music near the close.
The bright enamelled bird,
an unreflecting eye,
the grain of fingerprints
made clear as melting wax;
all individual lists
smoothed thin as unity.

Self-Criticism

That chirrup and scratch
I mistook for the song
of an unfamiliar bird
comes from metal on shoes
the night-soil workers wear
that catch on gravel, as
they master this hill
at shift's end.

My mind given over
to words due to the past
too little notices
changes in rhythm
of nature and policy.

I will go out soon
learning to read again
from the familiar notice,
declining the hill
To listen in discipline
for thrush-song
and swallow
the lie of the land.

Customs of the Province

The legends concerning
how we appear on the surface
of a lake or a much slid-on stone
are a requirement of faith.

In the pale early years,
a white costume was called for.
Now we mostly sleep and eat.

A forklift-truckful of bamboo
passes through the best of us
between darknesses.

In memory of the girl
whose skin was peach-blossom
we dip our hands and feet in pitch.

In memory of the tiger's anger
and our sad survival here,
we wipe our eyes with stained hands.

So you stare at us
and we return your gaze,
looking out sparingly
from behind twin moons of kohl.

Aspinall's Zoo

A four year-old's arm
raised to point out
the big cat slavering
on the long sloping bough.

That half term holiday,
our first year of teaching,
crazy with the shock of failure
we'd escaped to Kent.

How vulnerable the fences
seemed. The monkeys,
grieving disturbed adolescents,
threw shit at the laughing crowd.

It was that Sunday the hours change:
the evenings suddenly darker,
the animals' food unexpectedly late.

It took a decade to cope with the job,
another to study each other.

And every few years
these stories in the papers:
dismembered limbs,
loyal keepers' widows,
the stale excuses
of Lucky Lucan's friend.

Heritage

On the beach, elements
stutter in Greek—we're
pebble philosophers—

My father would pitch
a flat one spinning
to skip once, twice . . .
across uplifting water.

My sons and I
just feed the waves
like keepers tossing meat.

The Border

The queue might take an hour we're told.
Meanwhile, there's this form to fill, a relic of the recent past.
Currency, traveller's cheques, purpose of visit.
On the seat behind, you doze at last,
your glasses slipping down your nose,
the adventure discarded on your lap,
crumpled between your elbow and the seat.

It's your birthday and we're crossing to a new landscape.
This morning we saw harvests piled on rolling plains,
the chimneys of collective bakeries,
sheds where cattle live out secret lives indoors.
Now the afternoon unfolds on strips of field
where horses pull a plough
and hay's stooked in tidy decorated sheaves.

They put up the signs to Helsinki
the year that you were born. We watched
hesitant steps break into a confident
uneven run, the beginnings of self-control.
New choices will be made, unmaking the past,
and you, half-grown, rub your eyes awake
to a new country, another year in which to live.

The Tambourica Player's Wife

His stained fingers scratched
at the sympathetic strings.
Next to him the Romany
girl was singing the usual
tales of love's abandon and
abandoned love. Songs
of freedom: with wild eyes
like the skinny cats in the
locked Serbian church.

What lines his face,
I paid for too. So when
her voice twins with his
lamenting the times, it's
my heart floods. If not for
the nation saved, for the
future he stole, the island
cottage we should have had,
the smell of cypress after rain.

Revenants

It's this same train-rattled flat
   that we find shelter in, after
a Bohemian summer storm, presaged by
      dust-devils, cloud cover
and sudden corridors of wind.

The fretted rail of vine leaves
   that framed our balcony has gone.
The cane chairs we left behind, seatless,
      sprout long tendrils; they've lost
whatever strawberry or pistachio tint

made our neighbours covet them.
   Against cracked plaster and bared stone,
a pear-tree has wound round the towering beech
      in next door's abandoned garden.
Six meters up, it offers hard and tasteless fruit.

The broken-backed damp books
   are Pavel's, who kept the place
through the barely breaking winter of our
      London years. I take down
Hrabal's *I Served the King of England* and recall

a Saturday in Kew, the
   year that he could visit us;
how Pavel pulled his loping form up the
      wrought-iron spiral stair
to view the largest indoor plant in Europe,

touching the roof of the temperate house.
His vaulted cheekbones, his eyes
clear, blue, transparent as the sky through glass,
shaded by the foppish brim
of his unseasonal panama. Return won't bring

the great release we dreamed of
any more than exile did.
Faces altered by disease, age, or merely compromise
greet us back in Prague.
But summer storms end quickly here.

And, as in London, we seek
refuge in iron fantasies
of the Belle Époque: Petrin Hill's pastiche
of the Eiffel tower,
or the hall of mirrors where versions of our selves,

mis-shaped, repeat themselves
in mocking parallels.
The bright blue eyes of the soldier across from us
on yesterday's train
shone under the blue of his United Nations cap,

as Pavel's did at Kew.
Fates that ensnare enchant us first.
The sketchbook on your knee awaits defining lines.
Light and shade to draw the moment
from its labyrinth, to still a resisting heart.

The Secret Ministry

Šumplica Novakova laughed
as she zigzagged from queue to queue
in the cabbage market,
her last purchase always
the braided poppy-seed rolls.
Her bright silk blouses—
lilac, crimson or whichever colour
her hidden calendar required—
lightened the day,
when she broke and shared the eucharist
among carefully invited friends.

When a mate from the plant
made a fool of himself with a girl,
I'd invite him home for a meal.
He'd meet Jinka and the kids.
We'd drink a few beers, eat dumplings
and meat seasoned with a herb
that might recall his wife's name.
I gave absolution under my breath,
making a sign in the palm of my hand.

Now they've given the postal workers
museum back to the Cistercians.
I've a collar to wear and memos
from Rome about Mexican practices.
The lads are friendly enough,
but look at me
like a guy with something to sell,
some multinational's rep.

Last week, I saw Šumplica
in the marketplace,
finding the best fruit
as ever. Once, she whispered
what would not be silenced.
Now, she spoke out loud,
steadying her bicycle. It was
after all, love we ministered to
so no regrets. She laughed
as the pigeons scattered,
flying off God knows where.

Sunday Morning

Stevens, MacNeice and The Velvet Underground.
A lightness rising to a cloudless sky.
Too tired for sleep or love we drive together
out of numbness to a different town.
The long ponds where we used to feed the ducks,
the stretch of green that climbs to the cathedral,
the breakfast, the bookshop we trust will
take gravity from us, floating away.

But now the radio plays Haydn, a piece
in F sharp minor, contrived we're told
to solve a problem in the Esterhazy Court,
so in the last movement the players left
singly, snuffing out their candles, leaving
the last couple to hold the stage alone

That Year

She is steadying
her arm along the brick
wall of the railway bridge,

paused after hurrying
sweet swift uncounted drinks
with no reason, and sings

that without her looking
autumn has gone running
on its paths of orange;

only a vast moon
is left in the low
half-lit sky. An apple,

she says, sliced by
the slim-bladed trees.

Keeping Time : A Note on Some Sources and Dates

The march mentioned in 'In the palm of my hand' took place in June 2000, following shortly on the death of Chinese migrant workers being smuggled into Britain on a lorry. The busdriver, in July 2005, was George Paradakis. 'The TPA Bar' is in Denmark Street, London's Tin Pan Alley. The poem is set on the evening of June 30th 2007, the last day that smoking was allowed in enclosed public spaces in England.

'In the Street' is a free translation and abridgement of Pablo Neruda's poem 'Walking Around' from *Residencia en la Tierra* (1935). '*Y Habra Trabajo Para Todos*' (And There Will Be Work For All) was a slogan of Salvador Allende's Popular Unity coalition in the Chilean presidential election of 1970.

'The Milky Way' is set in the late 1970s, but looks back on the late 1960s. 'Melkweg' (meaning Milky Way) was a music venue in Amsterdam. The Dutch Provos were hippy anarchists whose 'white bicycle' scheme was as much a protest against private property as an environmental campaign. 'Mrs Wu' takes details of the young life of the Chinese Communist leader Zhou Enlai from the biography *Chou : Story of Zhou Enlai, 1898–1976* (1984) by Dick Wilson.

'The Cavalcantine Lure' is derived from Guido Cavalcanti's 'Sonnet XVIII'. 'Southerly' begins as a version of Yves Bonnefoy's 'A la Voix de Kathleen Ferrier' from *Hier Régnant Désert* (1958). Michaelangelo's drawing of 'Tityus' in the Queen's collection uses the outline of the pagan figure as the basis of a drawing of Christ's resurrection on the other side of the sheet.

The poem referred to in the latter part of 'For Ernest Seigler' is 'Happiness Makes Up in Height for What it Lacks in Length' by Robert Frost. 'The Folding Star', which takes its title from a poem by Collins (William rather than Billy), is loosely related to Horace's *Ode I xi* and to Tacita Dean's gallery film about Michael Hamburger, which was exhibited in Norwich Castle during the spring of 2007, a few months before the poet's death.

'Chez Haynes' is a restaurant in Montmartre. I first read about it in Edmund White's *The Flâneur* (2001). 'Echoes' is set in the academic year 1989–90. Zal Yanovsky played with The Loving Spoonful. The tape in 'Yes It Is' is The Beatles' *Past Masters*.

In 'Edit' the phrase 'but it would be wrong' is taken from reports of the Watergate cover-up. It was used to distance the president from wrong-doing. Some doubted its authenticity. The first line of 'Directive' owes a debt, initially unconscious, to Peter Porter's 'Mort aux Chats'.

'The Hammer' alludes to a passage in a reminiscence that Yeats wrote in 1920 for the liberal-nationalist review *Irish Statesman*: 'One day when I was twenty-three or twenty-four, this sentence seemed to form in my head, without my willing it, much as sentences form when we are half-asleep: "Hammer your thoughts into unity".'

In Communist Czechoslavakia to counter government quotas on numbers of priests, the Catholic Church ordained undercover worker priests, including women and married men. The two protagonists in 'The Secret Ministry' belonged to this group. The UN soldier in 'Revenants' was probably on his way to Bosnia. The locked Serbian church in 'The Tambourica Players' Wife' was in Dubrovnik; a few years later it had become an icon museum. Wallace Stevens, Louis MacNeice and The Velvet Underground were all responsible for lyrics with the title 'Sunday Morning'; the music referred to in my poem is Haydn's *Symphony No. 45* ('The Farewell').